Crazy

s

& Crafty Challenges

Published and distributed by
TOBAR LIMITED
The Old Aerodrome, Worlingham, Beccles,
Suffolk, NR34 7SP, UK
www.tobar.co.uk

This edition printed in 2009

Printed in China

ISBN: 978 1 903230 15 2

Text: Sandy Ransford
Illustrations: David Mostyn

INTRODUCTION

Can you turn water into wine? Get an apple into a narrow-necked bottle? Hold someone down in a chair with just the pressure of your little finger? Or perform astonishing feats of mind-reading and escapology? If you like playing tricks on people and can't resist a challenge, you'll have a lot of fun with this book.

Many of the stunts are very simple and require no equipment whatsoever. Some need everyday objects such as pencil and paper or string, which you'll have in your home. Some just show how your body – which you may think you know well – can fool you. (For example, one of them apparently makes one of your arms shorter than the other!) One or two tricks are more complicated, and require a bit of preparation before you astound the world with them – but you'll find they're well worth it!

Most of the tricks can be played on anyone. Some are a perfect way to entertain yourself; others are a great way of amazing – and amusing – friends and family, especially children. All you need do is follow the step-by-step instructions – and you'll be in great demand as an entertainer. Have fun!

Chicken Run

Can you get the hens into their coop without physically moving them or cutting the paper?

Props you will need:

Paper

Pencil

Postcard or business card

What to do:

1. You can recreate this drawing for yourself by tracing it on to a sheet of paper. Take care to make the distances between the hens and the dotted line, and the coop and the dotted line, the same as they are in our drawing.
2. Place the postcard or business card on edge on the dotted line.
3. Bring your face down to the postcard, so your right eye looks at the hens, and your left eye looks at the coop. And what happens? The hens trot into the coop!

Feet Together

You can stand with your feet apart and then move them together, can't you? Can you?

Props you will need:

A wall

What to do:

1. Stand with your feet apart, and your right foot and right shoulder touching the wall.
2. Now, still keeping your right foot and right shoulder touching the wall, put your feet together. Simple, isn't it?
3. Can you do it? Try it and see!

Balloon You Can't Pop

Is there such a thing as a balloon that won't burst when you stick a pin in it?

Props you will need:

A balloon
Adhesive tape
Scissors
A pin

What to do:

1. Blow up the balloon and knot its neck or tie thread round it so the air can't get out.
2. Cut off two small pieces of adhesive tape and stick them on the balloon to form a cross.
3. Stick the pin into the balloon through the centre of the tape cross. What happens? Nothing, the balloon doesn't burst!

Going Dotty

Do you ever see spots before your eyes that aren't there? Are you going dotty?

Props you will need:

Paper
Red and blue crayons or felt-tip pens

What to do:

1. Study the drawing on this page for a few moments. It's just a pattern of black squares that make up a rectangle, isn't it?
2. But when you've been looking at it for a while, dark spots will appear where the white lines between the squares intersect.
3. Copy the squares pattern on to a piece of paper, in red ink. Can you see green spots after a while?
4. Try the same pattern in blue ink. What colour are the spots now?

The Folding Stuff

How many times can you fold a piece of paper in half? Lots, surely. Try it and see.

Sheet of paper

What to do:

1. Get a sheet of paper, the thinner the better. Fold it in half.
2. Now fold it in half again.
3. And fold it in half again. Keep on trying.
4. After the fourth fold, it becomes more difficult, and after the sixth, it is virtually impossible. If you don't believe it, try it for yourself!

A Needle Can Float!

If you carefully place a needle on the surface of some water, will it float?

Props you will need:

A glass of water
A needle
A piece of paper tissue

What to do:

1. If you just place the needle on the water in the glass, it will sink. But there is a way of making it float.
2. First float a small piece of paper tissue on the water's surface.
3. Carefully place the needle on the tissue.
4. Wait until the tissue becomes saturated with water. It will sink, leaving the needle floating on the surface of the water.

Piece Of Pie

There's something very odd about this pie.
Somebody eats it when you're not looking!

Props you will need:

Nothing, except this picture

What to do:

1. Look at this picture. There's an apple pie on a plate and someone has cut out a slice and eaten it. There's plenty left for you!
2. Now turn the page upside down. Where's the rest of the pie gone? Someone has eaten it all and only left you one slice!

Whistle It Up

Can you whistle? If so, can you imagine anything that could prevent you from doing so? Try this.

Props you will need:

A lemon
A knife

What to do:

1. Cut the lemon in half and suck the juice out of it. Swill it round your mouth.
2. Now try to whistle. You are very unlikely to be able to do so!
3. You will probably be able to prevent someone else from whistling if you eat the lemon in front of them – if you can still bear to eat lemons!

Water Into Wine

Have you ever wished you could turn water into wine? Here's how to do it!

Props you will need:

A large enamel or pottery jug (not glass)

A plastic drinking mug

A wine glass

Blu-tack

Two small sponges

Absorbent kitchen cloths

Water

Wine

What to do:

1. Prepare the jug before you try to amaze your friends. Stick the Blu-tack on the bottom of the plastic mug and press the mug down firmly inside the jug. Make sure it will hold in place if you tilt the jug.
2. Pack the sponges and absorbent cloths round the plastic mug.
3. Carefully pour some wine into the plastic mug. Now you're ready to show off the trick.
4. Fill the wine glass with water and show it to your audience, telling them that you can turn it into wine.
5. Pour the water carefully into the jug so it goes on to the sponges and cloths and not into the plastic mug. It's a good idea to practise first to see how much water they will absorb and fill the wine glass accordingly.
6. Wave your hand over the jug and say, 'I will now change the water into wine.'
7. Tilt the jug and pour out a glass of wine – from the mug inside the jug!

Aristotle's Marbles

This trick was a favourite of the Greek philosopher Aristotle over 2,000 years ago.

Props you will need:

A marble

What to do:

1. Cross your middle finger over your index finger.
2. Put the marble on the table and touch it with your crossed fingertips. Instead of one marble, you will feel two!

Nosing Around

Can you write with your nose? Here's how!

Props you will need:

Paper

A pen or pencil

What to do:

1. This is a trick with which to bamboozle a friend. Bet them they cannot write with their nose (they'll agree), but say you can.
2. Then lay the pencil on the paper, bend your nose down towards it, and pretend to be writing. Of course, they won't believe you.
3. But – you have already prepared another piece of paper, on which you have written the words 'With my nose'. When your friend shows signs of getting cross with you, show them the piece of paper. Be prepared to make a hasty exit!

Hot Money

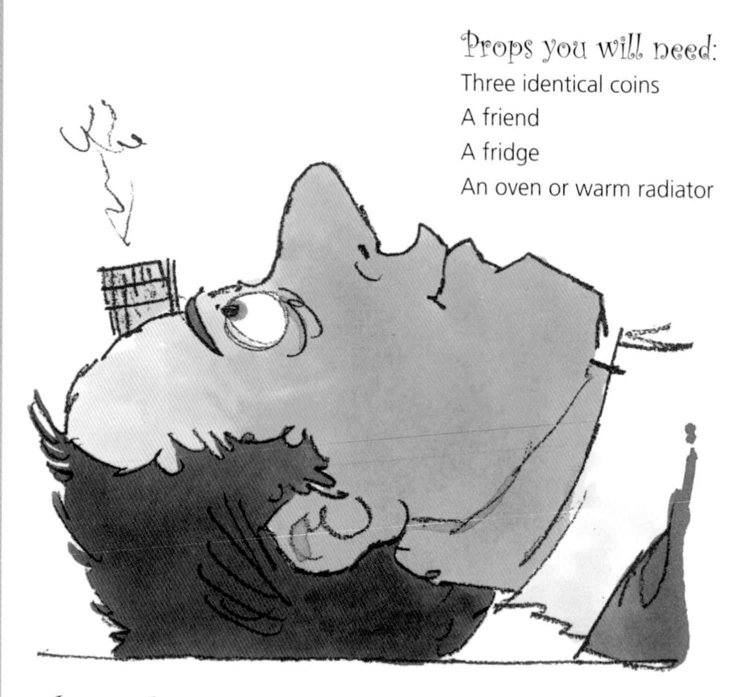

Props you will need:

Three identical coins
A friend
A fridge
An oven or warm radiator

What to do:

1. First prepare the coins. Put one in the fridge, and the other two either in a warm oven (not too hot) or on a warm radiator.
2. Ask your friend to lie down on their back, then put the chilled coin on their forehead. Ask them to think about its weight.
3. After a few moments, remove the chilled coin and replace it with the two warm coins, carefully balanced one on the other, so they feel like one coin. Ask your friend to think about the weight this time, and then ask them which of the coins was heavier, the cold or the warm. They will think they both weigh the same, even though (because there were two of them) the warm coins were twice as heavy.

Apple in a Bottle

I bet you can't get an apple in a bottle!

Props you will need:

An apple tree
A clear bottle
A piece of string

What to do:

1. This trick takes a while to prepare, but it's worth it. Tie a piece of string round the neck of a bottle, leaving some long ends.
2. In spring, when the apple blossom has gone and the little fruits are beginning to form, carefully slip a twig with a small fruit on it into the bottle. Tie the bottle on to the branch.
3. All you have to do now is wait until the apple has grown big enough to fill the bottle, but not so big as to break it.
4. When it has, cut the string and display your bottled apple. People will be amazed!

Straw Tease

Here's how to make a straw only you can drink through.

Props you will need:

A drinking straw
A drink
A pin

What to do:

1. First prepare the straw. Push the pin right through it about 2 cm from each end.
2. Put the straw in the drink and offer it to a friend. He or she will be unable to suck any of the drink up it.
3. Look puzzled, and say you will have a go. Hold the straw with your fingers over the two holes at the top. You will be able to drink from it without a problem!

Two-straw Tease

OK, you can drink through one straw, but can you drink through two?

Props you will need:

Two drinking straws
A drink

What to do:

1. Put the end of one straw in the drink in the glass, and its other end in your mouth.
2. Put one end of the other straw in your mouth also, but leave its other end out of the glass.
3. Now try to suck the drink up through the straw. It's impossible, isn't it?

Very Heavy Person

This trick will completely flummox all who see it.

1.

2.

Props you will need:

A friend who is bigger than you

What to do:

1. Stand as shown in the first picture, with your arms folded up to your chest and your elbows pointing vertically down to the ground. Ask your friend to lift you up by facing you, and cupping their hands under your elbows. If he or she is bigger than you, they should manage to do so without difficulty.
2. Then say that you can prevent your friend from lifting you, just by the strength of your mental powers. Without your friend noticing, move your elbows a bit further forwards.
3. When your friend tries to lift you a second time, they will be unable to do so. Of course, it is nothing to do with your mental powers, it is because you have subtly shifted your centre of gravity. But you don't have to admit it!

Extra-strong Egg

I'll bet you can't break an egg by squeezing it in your hand! Try it and see.

Props you will need:

An egg (uncooked)

What to do:

1. Put your hand right round the egg, and squeeze it. You think it'll break? Well, actually, it won't. Provided the shell isn't cracked, and you aren't wearing any rings, and you put an even pressure on the egg all the way round, it won't crack. Its shape is so strong it can withstand great pressure.

Climbing Through Paper

Can you climb through a sheet of writing paper? It sounds impossible, doesn't it?

Props you will need:

A4 size sheet of paper
Scissors
Pencil

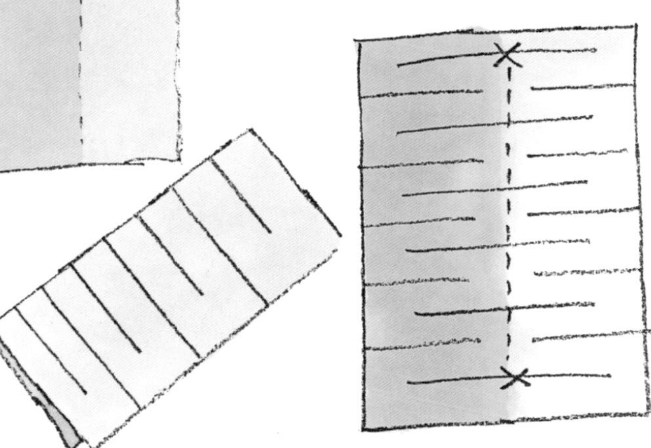

What to do:

1. Fold the sheet of paper in half lengthways.
2. Keeping the paper folded, cut it from alternate sides, but not right across, as shown.
3. Mark the top and bottom of the fold about 2.5 cm in from the edge.
4. Unfold the paper, and cut along the fold, between the marks you have made.
5. Carefully open out the paper – and you will discover you have made a ring big enough to climb through!

Electric Balloons

If you charge balloons with electricity you can have a lot of fun with them!

What to do:

1. Blow up the balloons and secure the necks by knotting them or tying thread round them.
2. Stroke the balloons with the fur, to charge them with static electricity.
3. You can now place some of the balloons either by a wall, or the ceiling, and they will stay there as if glued in place.

Props you will need:

Balloons

Fur of some kind

Fine thread

Drawing pin

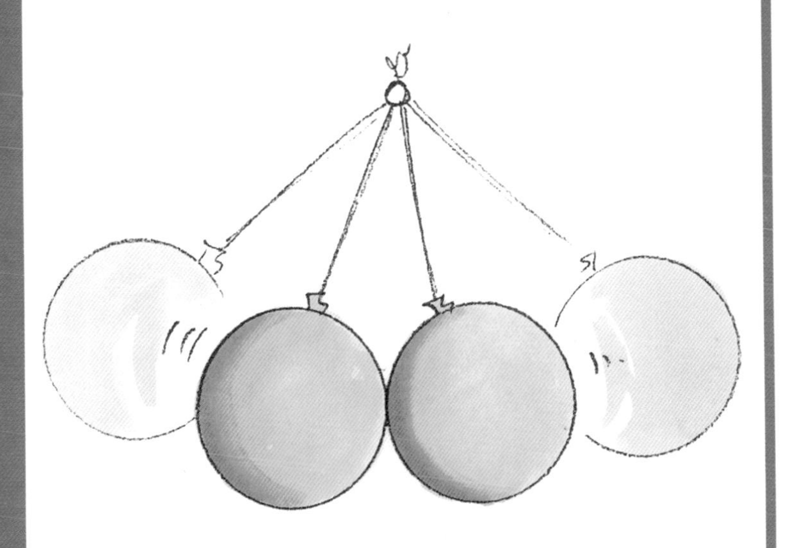

4. Tie threads round the necks of two of the balloons, and suspend them from the same point with the drawing pin.
5. The balloons will swing to and fro, repelling each other like the little swinging balls of an executive toy.

Test Your Strength

Here's another trick by which you can prove you are stronger than your larger friend.

Props you will need:
A broom handle

What to do:

1. Hold the broom handle with both your hands as shown.
2. Get your larger friend to stand opposite you and put their hands on the broom handle on either side of yours.
3. Tell your friend to push against the broom handle, and see if they can push you backwards. They will be convinced they can do this.
4. But, if instead of pushing back against them, you lift the broom handle upwards, they will find it impossible.

Unreachable

Challenge a friend to put their right hand where their left hand cannot reach it.

Props you will need:

Nothing!

What to do:

1. Challenge the friend, as above, and stand back to watch their contortions as they struggle to do as you ask.
2. When they can stand it no longer, show them how to do it. What, you don't know how? It's very simple. Just put your right hand on your left elbow!

Strong Fingers

Here's a simple way to prove how strong your fingers are.

Props you will need:
Nothing!

What to do:

1. Stand with your feet apart and fold your arms across your chest in front of you. Hold your hands so that the tips of your index fingers just touch.
2. Ask a friend to grasp your wrists in their own hands. Then bet them they can't pull your fingertips apart.

Weak Fingers

Having proved how strong your fingers are, now you can show how weak they are!

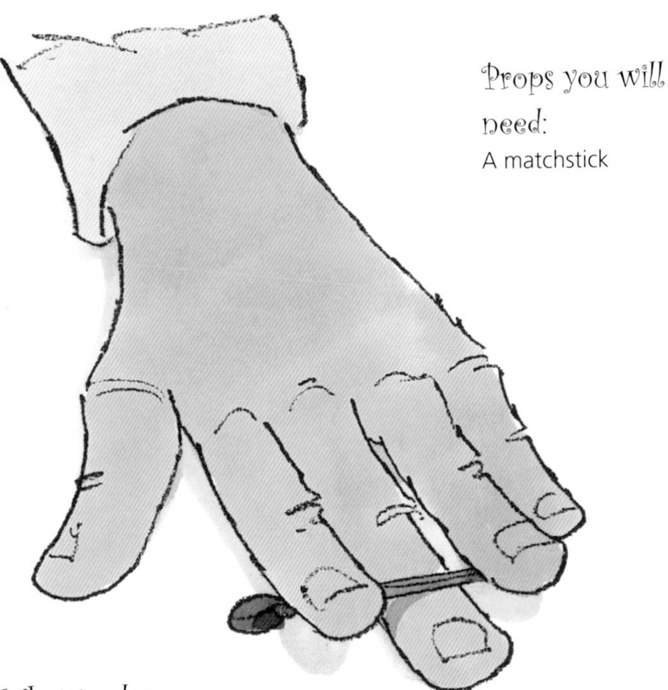

Props you will need:

A matchstick

What to do:

1. Put a matchstick over your middle finger and under your ring and index fingers, at the level of the joint nearest to your fingernails.
2. Now, keeping your fingers straight, push upwards with your middle finger and downwards with your ring and index fingers, and try to break the matchstick.
3. You're very unlikely to be able to do so unless you move the match up your fingers towards your hand.

Very Fishy!

Here's how to make a paper fish swim without touching it or blowing on it.

Props you will need:

Paper
Scissors
A pencil
Cooking oil
A large bowl of water, or a bath

What to do:

1. First draw your fish and cut it out. Note the circular hole at its centre, and the channel that connects the hole to the fish's tail.
2. Fill the bowl or bath with water.
3. Place the fish carefully on the surface of the water, so that its under side is completely moistened, but its upper side is kept dry.
4. Now you can challenge a friend to make the fish move without touching it or blowing on it. They will think it is impossible.

5. Then you show them it isn't. Carefully pour a large drop of cooking oil into the hole at the centre of the fish – and watch. The fish swims!
6. It does so because the oil spreads down the channel, thus propelling the fish forwards.

It Does Hold Water!

Would you think you can hold water in a glass with a postcard? Try it and see.

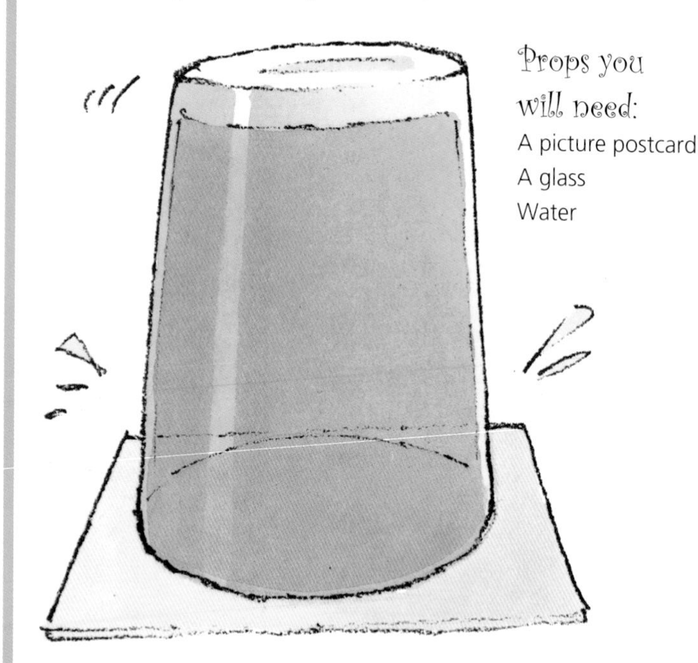

Props you will need:

A picture postcard
A glass
Water

What to do:

1. Fill the glass with water right up to the brim. Do this slowly so there are no bubbles on the surface.
2. Slide the postcard, picture side down, over the top of the glass. Take care not to spill the water, and also that you don't get any air trapped between the postcard and the water's surface.
3. Now slowly turn the glass upside down. If you're nervous, do this over the sink. But, believe it or not, the postcard will hold the water in the glass!

Round In Circles

Test your co-ordination with this trick.

Props you will need:

Nothing!

What to do:

1. Hold your hands up in front of your chest, with your index fingers pointing at each other.
2. Take your right index finger in a circle round your left index finger.
3. Then take your left index finger in a circle round your right index finger.
4. Now circle both fingers together – in opposite directions. Can you do it?

The Escapologist

Have you ever wondered how magicians perform escapology tricks? Well, here's one you can do for yourself, and amaze your friends at the same time.

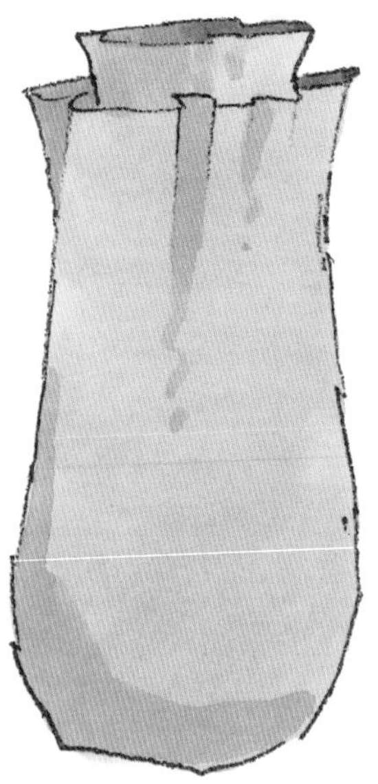

Props you will need:

Two large sacks
Two lengths of rope or string
A screen
An assistant

What to do:

1. Give your assistant a sack and watch him or her get into it.
2. Pull the top of the sack right over your assistant's head.
3. Hand a length of rope or string to a member of your audience and invite them to tie the neck of the sack so your assistant can't get out.
4. Put the screen in front of the assistant in the sack and slowly count to three.
5. When you get to three, remove the screen – and there is your assistant holding the sack over his or her shoulder! If the person who tied the sack examines it, they will see that the neck of the sack is still securely tied.

6. So – how do you do it? You may have noticed the list of props specifies two sacks. The assistant has one sack in their pocket, or pushed up their jumper, and as you pull the top of the sack over their head, they stick the top of the second sack up through the neck of the first. You hold the sacks to conceal this, apparently gathering the folds to help the member of the audience tie the neck. In fact, this person ties the neck of the second sack. So when the screen is in place, all your assistant needs to do is to climb out of the sack, put it in their pocket, and casually sling the tied sack over their shoulder. It's magic!

Knot Impossible

It sounds impossible – but when you know how . . . .

Props you will need:

A piece of string about 60 cm long

What to do:

1. Here's the challenge – tie a knot in the string while keeping hold of both ends of it. People get themselves into a terrible muddle trying to do it.
2. But this is how it's done. First, lay the string on a table where you can reach it easily.
3. Fold your arms.
4. Take hold of the right-hand end of the string with your left hand, and the left-hand end with your right hand. Don't let go.
5. Unfold your arms. Abracadabra there's a knot in the string!

Higher Than The Tallest Tree

This is a very silly trick that children love.

Props you will need:

Nothing!

What to do:

1. You make a bet with someone that you can jump higher than the tallest tree. If you are near some trees, you can point one out to them.
2. Your friend will know this is impossible, so will take on the bet, confident of winning it.
3. But they won't do so. Anyone can jump higher than the tallest tree – because a tree can't jump!

Suddenly Appearing Money

Props you will need:

A cup
A coin
A jug of water
A table

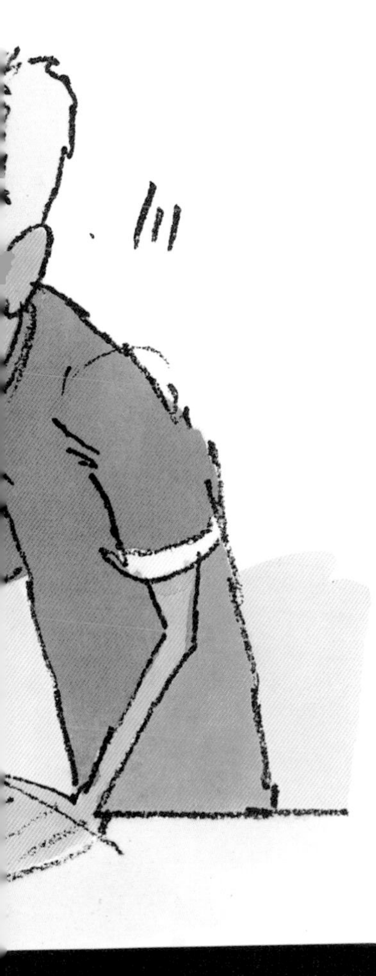

What to do:

1. Put the cup on the table and the coin in the bottom of the cup. Keeping your eye on the coin, move away from the table until you can no longer see it.
2. Make a note of where you are standing and then get a friend the same height as you to stand in the same place. (If they are not the same height, the trick won't work.)
3. Ask your friend if there is a coin in the cup. They will reply, 'No,' and when they do, tell them you can make one appear.
4. Make sure they don't move from the place where they are standing, and fetch your jug of water.
5. Pour the water from the jug slowly into the cup.
6. Your friend will give a cry of astonishment – for the coin will suddenly appear!

Hands Up!

In this trick you'll put your hands up whether you want to or not!

Props you will need:

A doorway

What to do:

1. Stand in an open doorway. Keeping your arms straight, press the backs of both hands against the door frame for half a minute or so. Time yourself with a watch, or count slowly up to 30 to get the time right.
2. Then relax your arms and step out of the doorway. What happens? Your hands go up into the air, whether you want them to or not!

Hands Down!

If you like a challenge, try this one.

Props you will need:

A broom handle or a cane

A matchbox

An assistant

What to do:

1. Put the broom handle or cane behind your knees, then hook your arms behind the handle and put your hands down on the ground in front of you.
2. Ask your assistant to put the matchbox on the ground in front of you.
3. Now try to pick up the matchbox in your teeth. Can you do it?

Putting the Finger On

This trick shows how amazingly strong your little finger can be. Or does it?

Props you will need:

A friend

A chair

What to do:

1. Sit your friend in the chair and ask them to tilt their head back so their chin is pointing upwards.
2. Then put your little finger on your friend's forehead and ask them to get up from the chair without moving sideways or wriggling about.
3. Amazingly, they will not be able to do so, and your little finger will be quite strong enough to keep them in the chair. In order to stand up, they first must move their head forwards, and your finger can prevent them from doing that quite easily.

Money Tease

Offer a friend some money – if they can pick it up the way you tell them!

Props you will need:

A friend

Some money

A wall

What to do:

1. Ask your friend to stand with their back to the wall, with their head and their heels touching it.
2. Put the money on the floor just in front of them.
3. Tell your friend that if they can pick up the money, without raising their heels from the floor or moving their feet forward, they can keep it.
4. You won't lose your money. It isn't possible to bend down and pick it up from that position without moving the feet.

Traffic Warden's Dream

Pity the poor person who drives the wrong way along a one-way street!

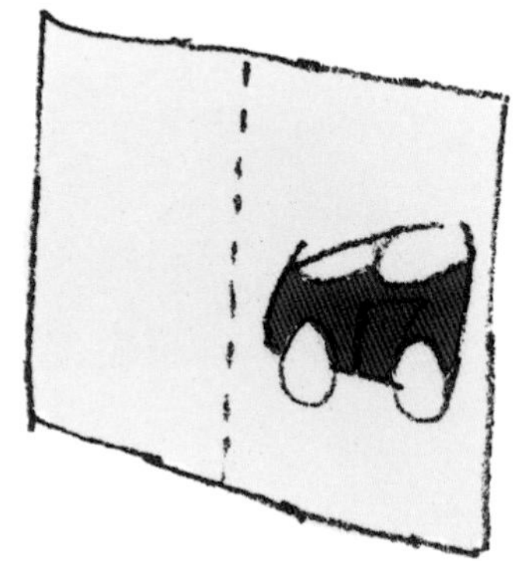

Props you will need:

A piece of paper
A pen or pencil
A straight-sided glass
A jug of water

What to do:

1. Fold the piece of paper in half. In the centre of one side of it, draw a car (or a motorbike, bus or other vehicle).
2. Stand the folded paper on the table like a greetings card. Place the empty glass about 10 cm in front of it, and look at your car through the glass. Note which direction it is travelling in.

3. Now make the car go in the opposite direction, without touching either the paper or the glass. Impossible?
4. Not if you know how! Simply pour water from the jug into the glass to fill it, and then look at the car again through the glass. It will be going in the opposite direction!

Mind Reading

Here's a trick you can play again and again, and still be sure of getting it right.

Props you will need:

A piece of paper
A pen or pencil

What to do:

1. Give a friend the pencil and paper and tell them to write down a three-digit number, whose digits decrease in value (such as 753).
2. Then ask them to write the same number backwards underneath it, and take the second number away from the first.
3. When your friend has worked out the answer, ask them what the last digit of it is.
4. You will then be able to tell them what the other two digits are.
5. How? Well, take the last digit away from nine, and this will give you the first digit. The middle digit is always nine. Easy peasy!

Mega Strength

Prove you are stronger than ten of your friends added together!

Props you will need:

A wall

Ten friends

What to do:

1. Face the wall with your arms out in front of you. Rest the palms of your hands against the wall.
2. Ask one friend to stand behind you and put their hands on your shoulders.
3. Then ask each of your other friends in turn to take up this position, one behind the other, with their hands resting on the shoulders of the person in front of them.
4. Then ask them all to push. You may imagine you'll be squashed against the wall, but you won't. Your arms will easily withstand the pressure of your friends, as each person absorbs the pushing power of the person behind them.

What Was That?

Bet a friend you can predict which word they will say next.

Props you will need:

A piece of paper

A pen or pencil

What to do:

1. Bet your friend you can predict which word they will say next, and tell them you have it written on the piece of paper. Say, 'I bet I can tell you which word you will say next.'
2. They will inevitably reply, 'What?'
3. At which point, you produce the piece of paper, on which you have already written, 'what'. You'll have won your bet!

Narrow Squeeze

Children will enjoy this challenge, which is to push yourself through a keyhole!

Props you will need:

A piece of paper
A pen or pencil
A keyhole

What to do:

1. Make a bet with someone that they cannot push themselves through a keyhole. They will readily agree with you. But then you say that although they may not be able to do it, you can. They won't believe you.
2. But it's very simple. Write your name on the paper, fold it up small, and push it through the keyhole. You have pushed yourself through the keyhole!

Shake a Leg

This is one of those odd tricks that no one can quite believe they can't do!

Props you will need:

A wall

What to do:

1. Stand close to the wall so your right shoulder and right foot are touching it.
2. Now bend your right knee and raise your right leg as if you were climbing up a stair.
3. No problem? Stand on your right leg again, with your right foot touching the wall.
4. Now bend your left knee and raise your left leg in the same way. Can you do it? You may manage a little hop, but it's very unlikely you'll be able to raise your left leg in the same way as you did your right leg.

Swing a Glass

Can you believe it's possible to swing a glass of water round upside down without spilling any?

Props you will need:

A wine glass
Water

What to do:

1. Fill a wine glass with water (or with wine, if you're very confident!) and hold it in your cupped hand, with the stem between your middle and ring fingers.
2. Without hesitating, quickly swing your arm round in a circle.
3. If you do it quickly enough, centrifugal force will keep the water in the glass, and you won't spill any. It might be as well to practise outside at first!

Cut it in Half

If you make a loop of paper and cut it in half, it will turn into two loops of paper. Won't it?

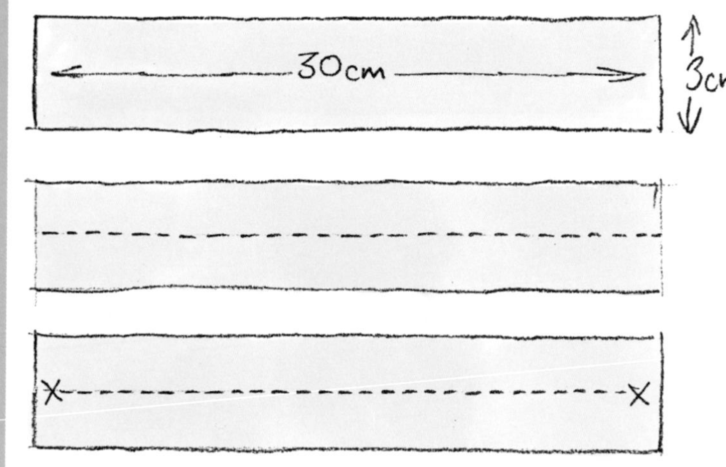

Props you will need:

A piece of paper
A pen or pencil
Adhesive tape
Scissors

What to do:

1. Cut out a strip of paper measuring about 30 cm long by 3 cm wide.
2. Draw a dotted line along the centre of the paper strip on both sides.
3. Draw a small cross at both ends of the strip on one side of the paper only.

4. Twist the paper once, then stick the ends together with adhesive tape, with the crosses facing each other. The crosses will then be hidden.
5. Then cut along the dotted line in the centre of the paper loop with the scissors. As you cut, the loop will start to divide into two. But as you get round to the beginning of the cut, what happens?
6. Instead of making two loops, your loop becomes one double-sized loop. It's all very strange!

Up the Pole

This is another clever little trick in which a weaker person is apparently stronger than a stronger one!

Props you will need:

A pole, such as a broom handle
A stronger friend

What to do:

1. Get the stronger person to hold the pole in a vertical position with both their hands. One hand should be near the top of the pole, and the other near the bottom.
2. Then get the weaker person to place the palm of one hand (the right hand if they're right-handed) against the pole, just above the other person's lower hand.
3. The stronger person should now try to push the pole downwards until it touches the floor. The weaker person has to push their hand against the pole to try to prevent them from doing so.
4. Who wins? Well, strangely enough, the weaker person will always win!

All in a Spin

Can you make an egg stand on end and spin round?
Try it and see.

Props you will need:

An egg
A saucepan
A cooker
Water

What to do

1. If you take an uncooked egg, hold it with its pointed end uppermost, and try to make it spin round, it is unlikely to do so.
2. Try hard-boiling it first, and then see what happens. The egg spins round!
3. You can use this to play a trick on someone, by hiding the cooked egg among uncooked ones, and betting them they can't make an egg spin round. You, of course, choose the cooked egg, and know you will always win!

Lifting Power

You can lift up a coin by sucking at it through a straw, can't you? Well, can you?

Props you will need:

A coin

A plastic drinking straw

A glass of water

What to do:

1. Put the coin on the table. Now try to lift it up by sucking hard through the plastic straw. Can you lift it?
2. Most likely you won't be able to. But dip the end of the straw into a glass of water and try again. You should lift the coin easily.
3. It's a good trick to try on a friend. Have a straw each, and secretly dip yours in water before you start. Your friend will be mystified why you can lift the coin when they can't.

Tongue-twister

Can you stick out your tongue and touch your nose?

Props you will need:

Nothing!

What to do:

1. Challenge someone to stick out their tongue and touch their nose. (Use those exact words, or the trick won't work.)
2. They will begin to squirm and wriggle, with their tongue stuck out and writhing around trying desperately to reach their nose with it.
3. But you tell them blithely that you can do it easily. How? Well, it's very simple. You stick out your tongue, and touch your nose with a finger! (This is why your phrasing of the challenge is important – you must say 'stick out your tongue and touch your nose'.)

Bottled Egg

This trick will baffle everybody!

Props you will need:

An egg
A milk bottle
Vinegar

What to do:

1. Your egg needs to be small enough to slide through the neck of the milk bottle. Put it in very carefully so it doesn't break.
2. Pour enough vinegar into the bottle to cover the egg. Leave it to stand for about 24 hours.

3. At the end of this time, the egg will have swollen quite a lot, and its shell will have become soft, though you can't see this. Carefully pour the vinegar out of the bottle, and rinse the bottle out with water to get rid of the vinegar smell.
4. You now have an egg much too large to get out of the bottle. Show it to people – who will be very puzzled as to how you got it in there in the first place!
5. After a day or two you will have to throw away the bottle and the egg, as they will be getting rather smelly, so make the most of the trick before they do so.

Eggs Squared

You can do amazing things with eggs. Read on!

Props you will need:

An egg
A plastic box, measuring approx. 4 x 4 x 4 cm
A saucepan
Water
A cooker
Kitchen paper
Cooking oil
A heavy weight, such as a large tin of tomatoes
A refrigerator

What to do:

1. First boil the egg for about ten minutes. Shell it carefully while it is still warm.
2. Pour some cooking oil on to kitchen paper and wipe it all round the inside of the plastic box, to grease it.
3. Put the egg, round end uppermost, into the box. Squash it down gently, until it's all in.
4. Put the lid on the box and stand the tin of tomatoes, or something similar, on it. Leave it until it is quite cool.
5. When it is cool, put the box in the refrigerator for half an hour or so.
6. Get it out and open the box. You will have a cube-shaped egg!

Vanishing Money

Well, it does, doesn't it? Though not always as quickly as this!

Props you will need:

A coin

A glass of water

A saucer

What to do:

1. Put the coin on a table.
2. Fill the glass with water until it is at least three-quarters full.
3. Stand the glass of water on top of the coin.
4. Then put the saucer on top of the glass.
5. What happens? The coin vanishes!

Lifting Device

Do you think you can lift a pile of books using just your breath? Have a go!

Props you will need:

A pile of books
A table
A small plastic bag

What to do:

1. Open the bag to make sure the sides don't stick together, then put it on the table, with the open end facing the edge of the table.
2. Put the books on top of the bag.
3. Blow into the bag – and what happens? The books rise up into the air!

Walking Coin

Can you make a coin move without touching it?

Props you will need:

A table
A tablecloth
A glass
A penny
Two larger coins, such as 50p pieces

What to do:

1. Put the tablecloth on the table. Then put the penny on the table, with the two larger coins on either side of it.
2. Stand the glass on the two larger coins. They should raise its base above the penny.
3. Now – the challenge is to get the penny out from under the glass without touching any of the coins or the glass.
4. How do you do it? You scratch at the tablecloth! The coin will 'walk' out from under the glass.

Slim Jim

Here's how to make someone lose a huge amount of weight in a moment.

Props you will need:

An old paperback book
A pencil
Two elastic bands

What to do:

1. Fold the book over lengthways.
2. Put an elastic band round the top and the bottom of it to hold it in place.
3. Draw a picture of a very fat person across the page edges, filling up the space as much as possible.
4. Remove the elastic bands – and what happens? The very fat person has suddenly become super-slim!

The Great Escape

Here's how to escape from an impossible situation.

Props you will need:

Two pieces of string, each about 1 m long

An assistant

What to do:

1. Tie one piece of string to your assistant's wrists – one end going round each wrist.
2. Loop the second piece of string round the first, then get your assistant to fasten the ends of it round your own wrists.
3. Now you are linked together, and the challenge is to get free without untying or cutting the string.

4. It seems impossible. You may try to climb over the string, or perform other complicated manoeuvres, but you will still be linked together.
5. So how do you do it? Get hold of the string that holds your friend's wrists together. Hold it in a loop, and take it over the string round one of your friend's wrists, then under the string towards you.
6. Spread the loop out and pass it right round their hand. Pull, and you and your friend are released!

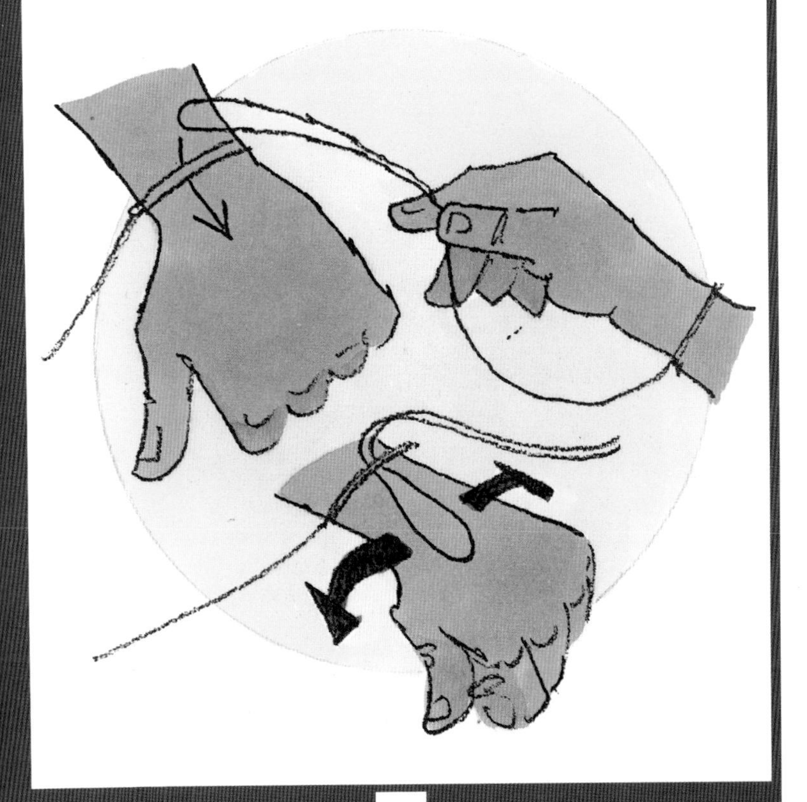

Honey, I've Shrunk My Arm!

Here's how (apparently) to make your arm shrink.

Props you will need:

A wall

What to do:

1. Stand facing a wall, your arm's length away from it.
2. Hold out one arm in front of you. Your fingertips should just touch the wall. Hold your arm so the palm of your hand faces downwards.
3. Holding your arm and hand straight, slowly swing your arm down and then back behind you. Then swing it forwards again.
4. Do your fingers still reach the wall? The chances are that they won't! Try the trick on a friend.

Game Plan

The winner of this game for two people is the player who picks up the last counter or coin, and if you know the strategy, you can be sure of winning every time!

Props you will need:

20 counters or coins

An opponent

What to do:

1. Lay out the 20 counters or coins on the table. Invite your opponent to go first, and to pick up one, two or three counters/coins.
2. You then have your turn, and pick up one, two or three counters or coins. Play continues like this, and the player who picks up the last counter/coin wins.
3. So what's the secret? It is to make the combined number of coins picked up at each pair of turns add up to four. So if your opponent (who must always go first – it looks like politeness but it's part of the strategy) picks up one, you pick up three. If they pick up two, so do you, and so on.
4. Providing you play like this, and your opponent starts, you will always win, since there will always be four coins left at the last go and your opponent can only pick up three.

Fruit Slices

Ready-sliced, unpeeled fruit sounds impossible, doesn't it? There's a simple way to do it.

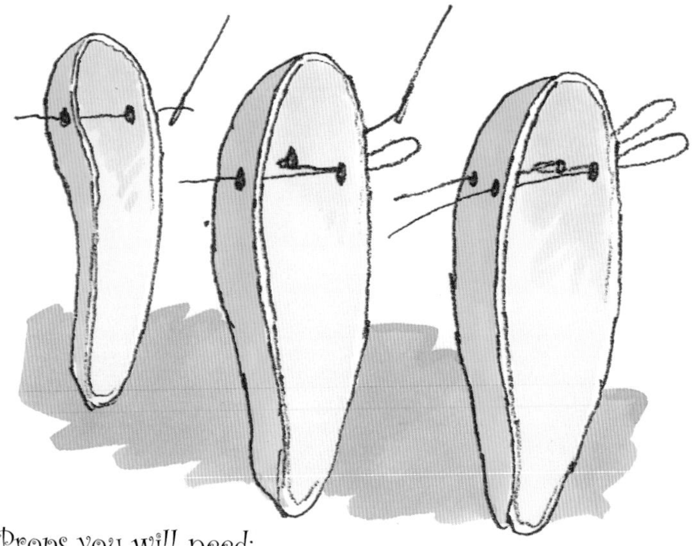

Props you will need:

A banana

A long needle

Thin sewing thread

What to do:

1. Thread the needle with about 20 cm of thread and push it into one of the 'seams' of the banana skin. Bring it out again at the next 'seam'.
2. Go in again at the same hole you just came out of, and come out at the third 'seam'.
3. Go in again at the same hole you came out of at the third 'seam' and come out at the first hole you made.

4. Pull the needle and thread out of the banana, and the thread will slice through the banana.
5. Move a little way down the banana and repeat the procedure to make the second slice.
6. Repeat as often as you want to make as many slices as you wish. When you have finished, you will not be able to see the tiny holes the needle made. But don't leave it too long before you play a trick on someone, or the banana will go brown.
7. Hide the banana in a bowl with others, and offer it to a friend. Watch their face as they peel the banana and see it fall apart into slices!

For Two Pins

This trick can make you see double – and possibly even treble!

Props you will need:

A sheet of paper

A pin

What to do:

1. Make two holes near the edge of the paper with the pin. They should only be about 1.5 mm apart.
2. Hold the paper close up to one eye. With your other hand, hold the pin behind the paper, close up to it.
3. Look through the holes at the pin. Then move the pin about 6 cm further away from the paper.
4. The one pin has suddenly become two!
5. If you make a third hole near the other two, to make a triangle shape, you may see three pins when you move your pin away from the paper.

Undroppable!

You wouldn't think that if you held a coin between two of your fingers, you would be unable to drop it, would you?
Try this trick and see.

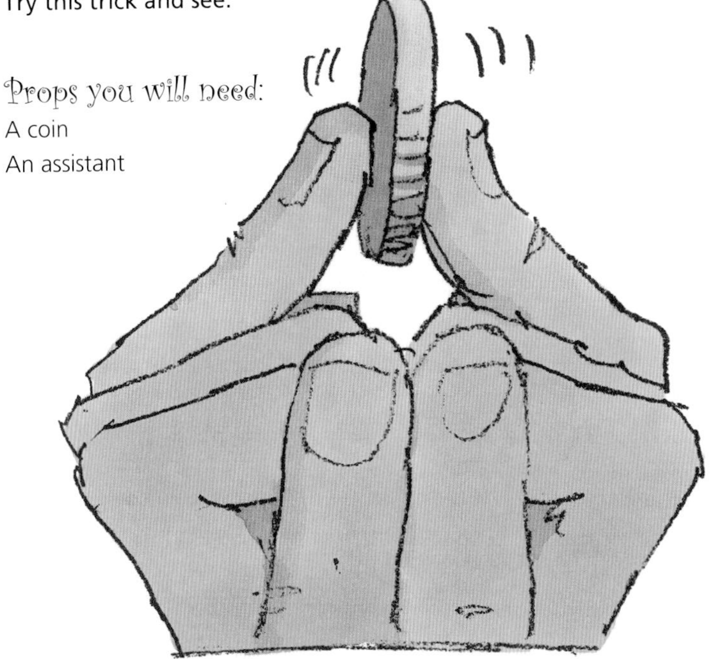

Props you will need:

A coin
An assistant

What you do:

1. Put your hands together, with your fingers bent down so the middle joints touch each other, all except for the ring fingers, which should stick up and touch each other at the tips.
2. Ask your assistant to put the coin between your ring fingertips, and hold it there.
3. The challenge is – without sliding the tips of your ring fingers apart, or moving your knuckles – can you drop the coin? It sounds silly, but it's very unlikely that you will be able to do so!

All Fingers and No Thumbs

This trick really tests your powers of co-ordination.

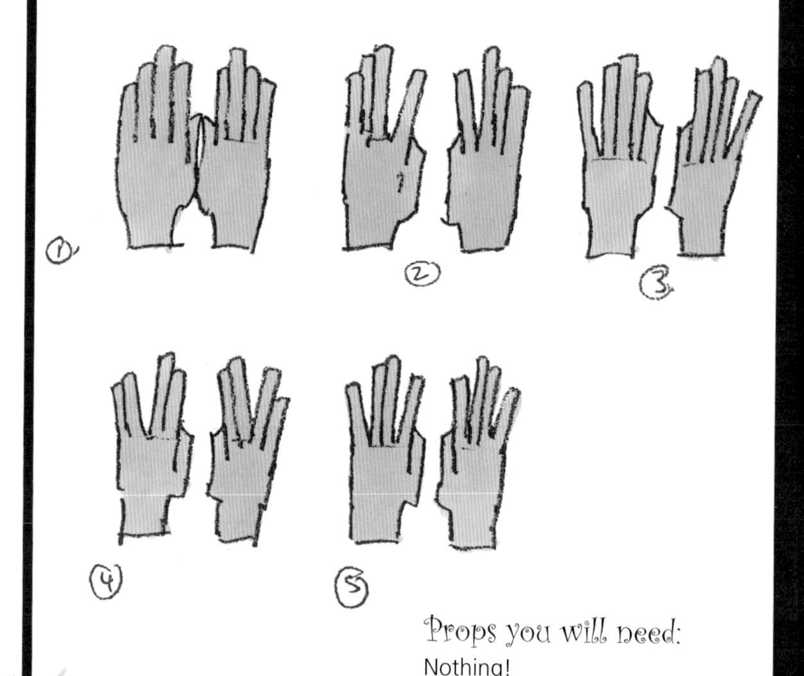

Props you will need:

Nothing!

What to do:

1. Hold both hands out flat in front of you, with your fingers together and the palms of your hands facing downwards.
2. If you're right-handed, start with your right hand, otherwise start with your left hand. Move the index finger away from the others, and then back again.
3. Then move your little finger away from the others and back again.

4. Now keep your index and middle fingers together, and your ring and little fingers together, and move the two pairs of fingers apart to make a V shape.
5. Move the pairs of fingers back together, then keep your middle and ring fingers together and move your index and little fingers away from them at the same time.
6. Run through the sequence again, and when you've got the hang of it, repeat all the moves with your other hand.
7. And when you've mastered that, try doing steps 4 and 5 with both hands at the same time.
8. Still with me? Here's the ultimate challenge. Do step 4 with one hand, and step 5 with the other, at the same time. If you can do so, your co-ordination is brilliant!

Very Wet Drink!

This sneaky trick might spoil a beautiful friendship, so choose your victim carefully! It's best played outside, as you will see.

Props you will need:

A plastic drinks bottle
A drawing pin
Water

What to do:

1. Make several holes in the bottom of the plastic bottle with the drawing pin.
2. Hold the bottle over the sink and fill it to the top with water. Screw on its top.
3. Hold the bottle by its top and mop up any water that runs down it with a cloth.
4. Offer a friend a drink, still holding the bottle carefully by its top as you hand it over.
5. They will unscrew the top – and get drenched! If you take the top off the bottle, or hold it anywhere except by its top, water comes out of the holes you made.